# Joseph Forgives His Brothers

Genesis 37, 39–45 for Children

Written by Robert Baden
Illustrated by Chris Sharp

ARCH ® Books
Copyright © 1996 Concordia Publishing House
3558 S. Jefferson Avenue, St. Louis, MO 63118-3968
Manufactured in the United States of America

D1367035

A man named Jacob had twelve sons
        In Israel long ago;
He loved the one named Joseph most
        And often told him so.

He made a richly woven robe
        That Joseph proudly wore;
His brothers didn't like the robe,
        Or that Jacob loved *him* more.

Then Joseph shared some dreams in which
His family bowed before him;
The brothers thought he'd gone too far
For them to just ignore him.

"I hate this boy," one brother said.
"He really makes me mad!
If Joseph disappeared," he said,
"I know that I'd be glad."

When Jacob sent him out where sheep
Were herded by his brothers,
One said, "Let's kill this dreamer now!"
But the oldest stopped the others.

"Don't kill him, please!" this brother said.
"Let's sell the boy instead.
We'll take his robe, smear it with blood,
And tell Father that he's dead."

So they sold Joseph to some men
Who came along that way;
And these men took him as a slave
To Egypt that same day.

Poor Jacob thought his son was dead;
His brothers soon forgot him.
But God kept Joseph safe with
Potiphar, the man who bought him.

With God's help Joseph did so well
Each job his master gave
That Potiphar soon liked him more
Than any other slave.

Then Joseph was accused of sin,
    And soldiers quickly jailed him.
His master's wife had lied, but
    Even then, God never failed him.


In prison, Joseph helped explain
    The dreams of men around him;
And when the ruler had a dream,
    He searched him out and found him.

The ruler, Pharaoh, shared his dreams
Of cows and stalks of grain;
And Joseph said, "This means the land
Will have a lack of rain.

"But first the cows and crops will thrive,
    And we can store up food;
We'll have enough to eat and more
    To sell when things aren't good."

The Pharaoh was so pleased by this.
He said to all the land:
"Hear this, my people … Joseph now
Is second in command!"

It happened just as Joseph said:
Crops grew for seven years.
But then came seven years of drought,
Of hunger, pain, and tears.

In Israel, Jacob and his sons
Had also seen no rain;
He sent them down to Egypt with
Some money to buy grain.

When Joseph saw his brothers bowing
    At his feet, he cried.
They didn't know him then, of course,
    Because they thought he'd died.

He told them who he was, forgave them,
    Took them in his arms.
"God turned your evil deeds to good;
    He kept me safe from harm."

The brothers hurried home and told
  Their father what had occurred;
Old Jacob said, "I can't believe
  This good news that I've heard!"


He and his family packed and left
  Their tents on desert sand
To live in homes much better now,
  In Egypt, Joseph's land.

Dear Parents:

All children feel jealous of brothers and sisters at times. Use this story as an opportunity to assure each (or your only!) child of your love. Talk about times that make family members feel jealous and angry. How can you share God's love and forgiveness in those times?

Explain to your children that even though Joseph was in terrible trouble—sold as a slave and put in jail—God worked through those trials to bring much good for Joseph and his family. Read Romans 8:28 with your family. "We know that in all things God works for the good of those who love Him, who have been called according to His purpose" (NIV®). Pray about a trouble your family has been having and ask God to work good through it. He will bless you—just as He blessed Joseph and his family.

The Editor